fight your
LIMITATIONS

Mame Yaa

ISBN 978-1-95081-834-1 (paperback)

Copyright © 2019 by Mame Yaa

All rights reserved. No part of this publication may be reproduced, distributed, or transmitted in any form or by any means, including photocopying, recording, or other electronic or mechanical methods without the prior written permission of the publisher. For permission requests, solicit the publisher via the address below.

Rushmore Press LLC
1 888 733 9607
www.rushmorepress.com

Scripture quotations marked KJV are from the Holy Bible, King James Version (Authorized Version). First published in 1611. Quoted from the KJV Classic Reference Bible, Copyright © 1983 by Zondervan Corporation.

Scripture quotations marked NIV are taken from the Holy Bible, New International Version®. Copyright © 1973, 1978, 1984 by International Bible Society. Used by permission of Zondervan. All rights reserved. [Biblica]

Printed in the United States of America

Contents

Introduction 5

Chapter 1: The Practicality of Marriage 7
Chapter 2: Taking Up Your Challenges/Responsibilities 28
Chapter 3: Don't Be Too Loud in the Marriage 37
Chapter 4: Avoid Competition in Marriage 54
Chapter 5: Respect Your Womanhood ... 64
Chapter 6: Woman as a Mother 73
Chapter 7: Family Limitations 78
Chapter 8: Our Focus in Marriage 87
Chapter 9: Conclusion 92

Introduction

Power control in marriage is a tiring job to do but going the extra mile for each other brings positive growth and the gains of a firm foundation. Cutting all suspicions away and showing sincerity towards each other fortifies the relationship. It is a process that joins your two characters together. Each other's character compliments and influence the other therefore the use of words, appreciation, love are powerful tools and driving forces that ships the marriage to a successful ground or shore.

Chapter One

The Practicality of Marriage

Marriage is a mystery and gift God gave to us and understanding ourselves make it simple. When God created the woman the man was asleep so it is God who will help you and lead you to find your wife. Marriage is:

- Is you the man finding your rib (the woman) that has the same similarities as you

- Love and togetherness built between the two
- The shared sacrifices on both parts
- Working on each other's character and weakness to perfection- thus you become one in mind and in decision-making, why? Because you are marrying each other's character and your whole being is for her and her whole being is for you.
- You both have made a covenant through blood

We have to learn to forgive each other because there would be fights and quarrels, this is to straighten and strengthen each other. If the life of the marriage is too quiet it will not survive because there is always work to be done somewhere, so having a boring marriage and neglecting problems will not help the marriage to survive. Sometimes we allow certain unnecessary problems that can easily be fixed through understanding to take control of the home and direct affairs, e.g. are cooking, dressing, neatness, comporting ourselves. When the joy in the marriage is cut short untimely death easily occurs because one party tends to endure too much pain and doesn't learn how to let go. The other party also tends to hold too much anger and too much of this is dangerous to the home and for the marriage. Remember that every time you love something you don't get angry at it. So many marriages are failing because there is too much pride between couples and their love and respect towards each other are affected and these same people become so arrogant to let those with skills teach them. They try to fix it themselves and they end up breaking. Some of these couples never had the platform to study or be taught by their parents or any adults about what marriage really is so they just enter into it because they grew up to see that others are doing it at a certain age. Others also marry as a form of fashion and show off. Yet still others also marry to avoid societal stigma.

Marriage is a journey, some parts are sweet and other parts are bitter but learning to blend the two will help solve certain problems. Marriage is not all about sex and beauty or how handsome my man is but it is about respect, honor, love, partnership, togetherness, humility and these will compliment your man or woman to be handsome or beautiful. In this kind of life if your character is not good how do you enjoy other things in your marriage? If you love your husband/

wife do not irritate them, this will make him or her leave you or the marriage. Treat them well and stop playing hide and seek with your spouse it is tiring trying to catch or find you. In doing this the confidence, faith and trust for each other would be shaken. Let us learn to stay with our wives and husbands alone and stop cheating it is a number one home wrecker. If you don't know about Christ, how would you survive in your marriage? Learn to let your partners have peace in the marriage.

"Love is patient, love is kind. It does not envy, it does not boast, it is not proud. It does not dishonor others, it is not self-seeking, it is not easily angered, it keeps no record of wrongs." – 1 Corinthians 13:4-5

"Marriage should be honored by all, and the marriage bed kept pure, for God will judge the adulterer and all the sexually immoral." - Hebrews 13:4,

In Genesis 2: 18- God said it is not good for man to be alone. I will make a helper suitable for him.

Wherefore they are no more twain, but one flesh. What therefore God hath joined together, let not man put asunder." - Matthew 19:6

Ecclesiastes 4:9, "Two are better than one, because they have a good return for their labor: If either of them falls down, one can help the other up. But pity anyone who falls and has no one to help them up. Also, if two lie down together, they will keep warm. But how can one keep warm alone?"

- Man you cannot leave alone and it is not good for you to do so, please respect and love your wife. See, God created you first and gave you sense and knowledge so that you can give a name to everything that He has made. He definitely and intentionally put you in charge because you are his image, therefore He made you to rule over his works and to be the boss over them and only God himself will be your head. There is power in your mouth when you speak and give names to things they appear to be so. Have you noticed that every negative name that you call your wife with, so shall she be for you until you work on her to become what you desire or need?

Everything that God created he gave it you and said till the land and keep it. When it came to woman he took your rib to make her so that you will feel the invisible pain of your lost rib when you hurt her. Every time you try to break her; you have broken your one rib so the pain you first feel jumps straight to your heart before your mind even starts thinking on what to do. Since you cannot break your rib physically why break it spiritually. A broken rib doesn't make you look manly or give your manliness back to you, it makes you look weak and vulnerable. To me, you look very funny if you beat your wife for her wrongs, it is just like taking your own rib and hitting it on a stone, you feel the pain in the end yet you will not stop even after screaming it hurt. When God was creating the one woman for you he made you sleep making it a mystery to you how he did it, why, because he put something in the woman, a secret thing that only you can discover so if you don't source it out to enable you work on the purpose for being here on earth then don't blame anybody. Because if you were heading a company you will look for those who will help you build the company and assign work to them according to their abilities.

So ought men to love their wives as their own bodies. He that loves his wife loves himself." - Ephesians 5:28,

"Husbands, love your wives, even as Christ also loved the church, and gave himself for it." - Ephesians 5:25, KJV

Give good names to your wife so that she becomes what you call her; if you call her sweet and handle her sweetly, she will become sweet for you. If you call her prosperity and uses her skills to your advantage she would be prosperous for you but if you call her lazy or crazy and treat her lazily or crazily, oh! Watch this; that is what you would get. So my point is name her and work on her to become the fertile land you want and then your harvest will be plentiful. Because of the power you have in your mouth everything you named from the beginning so it has been till now. Why abuse your creative power to build and grow.

In Genesis 1:27-29- God gave the scepter to rule on this earth to man and the command to be fruitful and multiply to both the man and woman. So man, you have the power to rule over your wife's negativity and be creative enough to change it at your command of wisdom into positivity but not to beat her or hail insults at her for the change you need, it will not work unless you act wisely. When you close from work try to leave work activities at the office and assume your role as husband in the home this even relaxes your mind.

"A soft answer turns away wrath: but grievous words stir up anger." - Proverbs 15:1,

With all lowliness and meekness, with longsuffering, forbearing one another in love." - Ephesians 4:2

You want your wife to respect you then be tactful about it; speak to her respectfully;

making her feel a sense of belongingness and all the while pointing at her mistakes, I tell you she would not talk back to you angrily or nag but she would seek for your opinion in how to solve the problem. But if you try to make her feel like she is nothing when she is your wife, then you the man stupidly are in for trouble. God told Adam (man) to take over and control everything and by this everything the woman does honors you (husband) including how she dress, talks, and she is your food to eat from and your well to drink from so if you cannot be content and treat her right then you don't have a head.

Proverbs 5:19, As a loving hind and a graceful doe, Let her breasts satisfy you at all times; Be exhilarated always with her love

"Live joyfully with the wife whom thou loves all the days of the life of thy vanity, which he hath given thee under the sun, all the days of thy vanity: for that is thy portion in this life, and in thy labor which thou takes under the sun." - Ecclesiastes 9:9,

You are the man and everything you touch must be fruitful for yourself so if you cannot treat your vine right to be fruitful then you have a problem. So start fixing yourself first before you start fixing your wife.

- Woman, you are the helper the one who receives from the man and act it out. Whenever you try to fill the man's position don't you realize how tired you get, and how messed up your marriage and home becomes.

You start to nag a lot and scare your husband and children with your attitudes; how then are you going to be happy this way. Because you help manage the affairs in your marriage when things are not going well, you have the right to voice your problems out. But you, you are the man's rib, why would you break yourself to hurt the man because of something the man did which didn't go in your favor or are you pulling an attitude to hurt his pride, don't you feel so much pain when you do this. Enjoy yourself being the woman and let your man pamper and love you.

"House and riches are the inheritance of fathers: and a prudent wife is from the Lord." - Proverbs 19:14,

Colossians 3:18, "Wives, submit yourselves unto your own husbands, as it is fit in the Lord."

- Every woman is special and wonderful in the sight of God and man. It takes a woman to be able to understand the perfect creation of God.
- It also takes a woman for the world to be full through procreation
- It takes a woman to see the softness of God's creation
- Every woman is a comforter and helper for her husband
- It took a woman for marriage to be established.
- In proverbs 12:4, a woman is the crown for her husband
- It also took a woman for the savior to be born.

This goes to say how important a woman is in this creation and world that we are in. imagine this world was full of men and animals; think of how the world would be like and how it will feel like.

This is how important the world needs a woman to grow or replenish.

- Read this text below and judge where you stand in your marriage and if it is not good, change your immediately otherwise your fragrance will smell poisonous.

Ecclesiasticus 25:13-25- this is found in the Sirach version

[13] Any wound, but not a wound of the heart! Any wickedness, but not the wickedness of a woman!

[14] Any suffering, but not suffering from those who hate! And any vengeance, but not the vengeance of enemies!

[15] There is no venom worse than a snake's venom and no anger worse than a woman's wrath.

[16] I would rather live with a lion and a dragon than live with an evil woman.

[17] A woman's wickedness changes her appearance, and darkens her face like that of a bear.

[18] Her husband sits[h] among the neighbors, and he cannot help sighing[i] bitterly.

[19] Any iniquity is small compared to a woman's iniquity; may a sinner's lot befall her!

[20] A sandy ascent for the feet of the aged—such is a garrulous wife to a quiet husband.

[21] Do not be ensnared by a woman's beauty, and do not desire a woman for her possessions

²² There is wrath and impudence and great disgrace when a wife supports her husband.

²³ Dejected mind, gloomy face, and wounded heart come from an evil wife. Drooping hands and weak knees come from the wife who does not make her husband happy.

²⁴ From a woman sin had its beginning, and because of her we all die.

²⁵ Allow no outlet to water, and no boldness of speech to an evil wife.

We set traps for ourselves through our fears that our spouses will do something behind our backs and because of our anger and jealousies we stir up fights and we express all our emotions without any control over them. Break yourself away from suspicion and stop hearsays. Those people who are lying to you want to break up your home so be sensible. Sometimes pause a little to check the root cause of the other spouse behavior and uproot it from the very source.

Proverbs 31:11-12, "The heart of her husband doth safely trust in her, so that he shall have no need of spoil. She will do him good and not evil all the days of her life."

In a family where the wife is not respecting and submitting to her husband, that house is full of arguments, fights, complains, abuses, etc. – it is a difficult family. Fights and arguments between a husband and wife arise because the wife is rising to be head of the man – she is disrespecting and not submitting to her husband. A man is naturally a head, a God given role, therefore when another head rises in a family where the man leads, there will be a fight.

Titus 2:5, To be discreet, chaste, keepers at home, good, obedient to their own husbands, that the word of God be not blasphemed."

- Women when we stand by our men both in public and in the private times we:

  ➢ build them up in their self-confidence in their person as men
  ➢ We reflect them positively to others.
  ➢ We command their respect from others
  ➢ We become their advisors who they listen to

- We become their companion; they would love to take us any where
- They become confident because they know they are needed.
- Don't give bad advice to them; you will scare him away from you
- We have the convincing tongue to speak to our husband's heart to bring about good change through respect
- When you are good to your husband you become your husband's eye to see problems and fix them.

Chapter Two

Taking Up Your Challenges/ Responsibilities

Most men are now irresponsible in the homes and so the women have taken the lead to direct affairs for them. The women are helpmeet/ helpers to the men the men are to sweat and do the job but now the women are doing the sweating and because the women are the weaker vessels they tend to get tired quickly. Even now in most job places most women work hard labor more than the men to put food on the table for kids and their homes, and sometimes their extended families this is because they do it well. Our men, stop drinking and avoiding responsibilities and take up your mantle to earn your respect. Some men are really responsible but they are getting few. Usually, we are supposed to check our weaknesses and fix them but why the delay?

There are differences in character when two people meet and it gets to a time in marriage when submission and pampering gives you the power to direct the home. There can never be two captains in your home. One have to submit. It is a give and take affair in a home. Love comes with pampering and being firm on decision making and submission also given should be done with pampering and through respect. If these positions are switched the home will be in chaos or will be collapsed. Both have a point somewhere but there have to be a compromise otherwise you will lose your home. Be wise to know when to pamper when necessary or demands call for it. And when to change the course of affection when things are going wrong through prayer and sweet talk. Not through nagging. Sometimes silence is your weapon.

The woman is like a worker who has been hired into a company. You will have to follow the directions and work assigned to you. The work has its own ethics to follow. You can never climb over the owner of the company to be his boss. But what you do is to work for promotion. Because you want to be promoted you will invest all efforts and knowledge and time into it. You will also exercise good speech to earn your keep and respect. This is similar to the home, when you let your husband feel that genuineness and submission towards him by letting him be in charge and direct the affairs, you will definitely earn your respect with him. You the woman handle and manage the affairs of the home and with the resources that are provided by the man. If these positions are switched there would be a gap. Your way of handling these resources well will either command your respect from the man or not. If you abuse it how do you want to be paid? All you have now would be excuses. There would be no happiness. Don't be too proud to learn and grow in your marriage by learning from each other, and women don't be lazy in the home. Look for the troubles that need to be fixed immediately, especially, the ones your husband usually complains about. We need to watch the words that we say to each other. It should rather build us than to destroy us. Each one should be responsible enough not to put out or quench the other's fire otherwise the coldness will break the marriage. Treat well what you have and keep it.

- Women are creative thinkers and far-sighted people, they think into the future and help plan for the future of her home. The well- being of her home with or without the husband's help are put into consideration. She works to become the mentor for her children. She is open and builds an easy communicative relationship with her children and others. She values her relationships to the point where she starts nurturing them to grow as she develops a strong sense of understanding through her drive and motivation for the family. This enables her to acknowledge the differences in character in her home and she works to draw out their different performances for the good of the family. She nurtures their skills and uses it to lead her members to the right direction of life.

- Women naturally are great listeners, they take the time to listen to the individual problems present at home and from her kids and husbands. We listen and stand by our people whether they are right or wrong. From a view point we show our appreciation for the trust shown to us and then make reliable decisions and solve problems.

We do well when we gain the trust of others.
- Women love being a part of the team at home, including her in the decision making at home grows and increase her passion, enthusiasm, capacity, ability, skills, and her immense ability to serve everyone and she does it with so much joy.
- Another of her skill is multitasking- we respond and react easily to problems and challenges and usually we know the solutions to these problems. In fact we are motivated by these challenges, because in this our desire to problem solving arises.
- Man – you are the symbol of authority in the home therefore you cover your home with your spirit. So when you bless your home it will be blessed and when you curse your home so it will

be. So if you the head cannot handle your home well then your home will be led astray.
- God gave you (man) the ruler ship to rule and subdue and multiply so if you misplace your rights you will be ruled over and you will lose your respect in the end.
- Have you noticed that anytime your children are not under your rule and under your covering, their lives become messed up? It is your responsibility to watch over these children you bring to the world so please stop these divorces.
- You lay down the vision, plans, and the helpers (women) will process it with the resources you provide. It is your duty to monitor the progress and success because you are the leader of the team.

- You are not supposed to compete with your wife over anything otherwise you will just be competing with yourself. It is meaningless
- It is like precious oil poured on the head, running down on the beard, running down on Aaron's beard, down on the collar of his robe.- see the blessings poured onto you runs down to your wife and to your children. It is not this way; that the woman get the blessing and it is poured down to you.

Chapter Three

Don't Be Too Loud in the Marriage

"Set me as a seal upon your heart, as a seal upon your arm, for love is strong as death, jealousy is fierce as the grave. Its flashes are flashes of fire, the very flame of the LORD. Many waters cannot quench love, neither can floods drown it. If a man offered for love all the wealth of his house, he would be utterly despised." - *Song of Solomon 8:6-7*

"With all humility and gentleness, with patience, bearing with one another in love, eager to maintain the unity of the Spirit in the bond of peace." –*Ephesians 4:2-3*

There are too much show off nowadays in the process of marrying our partners that we skip the most important issues prior to the marriage. We end up scaring our partners after these so called lavished marriages and ceremonies are completed. Mostly this kind of marriages break easily. There are so much characters formed in our partners that we failed to take notice of all in the name of love and this warning signs were seriously ignored just to have that man or woman.

"Let the morning bring me word of your unfailing love, for I have put my trust in you. Show me the way I should go, for to you I entrust my life." - *Psalm 143:8*

➢ Before marriage

Young ladies and women/men who are seeking marriage try as much as possible to submit themselves to their fiancés and boyfriends/girlfriends trying their possible best to lay the attention on themselves with the effort of the men/women seeing how attractive and good they can be to them as wives/husbands. During their relationship journey, these women/men try so much not to offend their partners so that the attention on them is not lavished on someone else. Whatever their partner request, to the abilities of the man/woman, he/she would do it, and he/she would even go to the extent of apologizing even if he/she is not at fault. Making the men/women feel proud and think they are on top of their game. Some of these men/women would defy the laws of nature and their family to stick to their partner until their married.

- "Let love and faithfulness never leave you; bind them around your neck, write them on the tablet of your heart. Then you will win favor and a good name in the sight of God and man." - *Proverbs 3:3-4*

➢ After marriage

The submission and respect between the woman and the man begins to fade away since they know they have now secured their positions beside their partners. Things the man used to do before now seems to offend the women easily and things the women used to do until now arouse an unknown anger in the man. And this feelings are mostly shown or transmitted through communication.

- What has changed? One may ask.

Before marriage, the only objective in the mind and the eyes was marriage and how we can get away from home and also quench the rumors and negative thoughts in the hearts of family members and friends as to when we are getting married. So therefore, we are somehow blindsided towards the man/woman we get involved with and sometimes we only hear how handsome/beautiful or caring the man/woman is from our friends and families especially, from our mothers. We ourselves tend not to really notice our partners for who they are, we only see them through what they can do and how people talk about them to us, feeling very proud of what we hear, we rush forward with all our efforts and when we enter into that agreement of marriage then we tend to notice how long the man's nose is and how it doesn't suit the face when he is chewing on something. And this is when the man also realize how clumsy the woman is.

So we have married the one we chose, so what? Are we regretting it now that we have worked to achieve that goal?

"Owe no one anything, except to love each other, for the one who loves another has fulfilled the law." - *Romans 13:8*

It will seem so funny, struggling so much to buy a car and then putting the car aside to walk to work just because the car is not nice or does not suit our taste, then in the first place why did you but it?

It will also seem so funny when you struggle to build or buy a house and then leave that house to rent a place or sleep outside, what is the sense in that?

In these two scenarios there is something similar, we needed it so bad that we did not even take our time to examine it or we just wanted to show off that we can also do that which others have done.

Let's come back to our topic; between these scenarios, why did you marry your wife or husband? For show or to release stress?

Marriage is a journey which comes with age involving two people along that journey. Walking on this journey alone cannot be called marriage. At a point in time you would want to turn back time or would want to go back to where you started from because the road ahead of you is not that clear, but this is when the other person comes in to encourage you, hold your hands with smiles and lead you on with the hopes of being by your side forever till the age ends for the both of you.

Ecclesiastes 4:9, "Two are better than one, because they have a good return for their labor: If either of them falls down, one can help the other up. But pity anyone who falls and has no one to help them up. Also, if two lie down together, they will keep warm. But how can one keep warm alone?"

On this road, there are gravels, stones, a narrow path, a cross road and a wide road; all these are things to be walked on and they all cause pain as you walk on them. Sometimes the tired party would want to give up, but the one who is with strength has to lead the other on with smiles and hope.

Marriage- a journey where you really do not know where you are heading towards but you just walk on with the hopes of getting somewhere positive. But what if you are both tired to continue walking on this road? "Two are better than one, because they have a good return for their labor: If either of them falls down, one can help the other up. This is where communication between both becomes critical and very sensitive. Some problems may arise but if the agreement made between the two becomes shaken the joy of the journey will not be realized.

In proverbs 15:4, A wholesome tongue [is] a tree of life but perverseness therein [is] a breach in the spirit.

1 Peter 3:7, You husbands in the same way, live with your wives in an understanding way, as with someone weaker, since she is a woman; and show her honor as a fellow heir of the grace of life, so that your prayers will not be hindered.

On this journey and on this rough patch, a sound advice and a sound counsel between the two will bring healing to each other. Two partners cannot be leaders on this road, one has to lead and the other follows. But sometimes the one in the lead's advices may not be sound so what do we do then? Bible says and the two shall be one. Which means one in thoughts, decision making, and focus. Let's think from this perspective- as one person your decisions are not always right, sometimes you have to start all over again and other times you are very sure of what you are doing with a strong conviction that it is leading to good. Even so you still weigh your decisions to know which one is best to approach before you leap into action.

So coming to the sense of two, you are not the only one walking on this road so that you think for yourself alone, you would have to consider the other person too in the decision making between the two. And without the two willing to sacrifice something there would not be peace or a proper understanding. If each one feels that what I am saying is the best and that the other has to follow, there would be no sense and the result would be foolishness.

We must take keen notice of the road we walk on in marriage together because it will influence our decision making in the future and sometimes it will call for sacrifice. It is our choice to exercise this to have a good marriage that we can enjoy.

Before you took the journey to marriage, you know or realize that the road or place you first were, was not good and so you embarked on this together, where ever you started from if it was a good place you would have stayed there, so why go back after the journey of marriage have been embarked on.

Each partner should be able to understand the strength and weakness of the other so that in those difficult time you can look back on how much the other has influence your life; if it is for good then that is the strength but if it's for bad then that is the weakness so it is time for the person to allow the strong party to contribute in decision making with character and attitude of listening instead of thinking that the other party would take their position. As a man, the woman would only take your position if you give your responsibilities to her to perform and when she is able to do it and do it well then she begins to look down on you. But if you allow her in decision making but listens to her with much love and understanding and also use her decisions as part of your responsibilities to achieve the goals, you would earn her respect and submission and she would always want to look up to you.

So on this journey of marriage, it is not about who the leader is but how you work out your understanding between the two and make each other feel respected.

Age gap and experiences

Considering the age gap and the experiences of the individuals in marriage is also very necessary. Some men or women think because they are older in some years than their spouse,they have to be in so much control but let me tell you it does not work at all! Others also use their experiences in live such as previous marriages, bad friendship encounters, or bad family background as an excuse to bring trouble to the home.

Let's face fact in your decisions to take this journey together, you were conscious of the age gap and the bad experiences yet you took the journey together. Don't you think it is about time you change that perception and attitude?

There are some who think the younger spouse may be wiser than them and may tend to look down on them so they decide to use the age gap to bully them by attacking almost everything they do except for sex. But this is the time to allow the spouse to be a part of you and bring to you the advantage of standing out tall by applying that wisdom tactfully without making the other person feel used even though they are your spouse. And there some spouses who focus on their partner's mistakes as though they are lying in wait to notice as soon as possible mistakes that look similar to their previous spouses' mistakes. And then they take the misunderstanding from there. But isn't it the time to forgive the other and yourselves and learn how to fix problems? Learning to complement each other and giving compliments sometimes help strengthen the relationship in the marriage. Remember that marriage is the name on the partnership and agreement but the add-ups are what make it worthwhile (friendship, love, kindness, sharing, respect etc.) you can love your friend more than yourself, why can't your love your spouse? You can share your problems and thoughts with your friend why can't you share it with your wife? Even if your spouse cannot contribute to the solutions like your friend will do, at least sharing with your spouse brings about sense of security and belongingness.

Chapter Four

Avoid Competition in Marriage

Amos 3:3- Do two walk together, unless they have agreed to meet?

You are one so be yourselves and stop competing with each other. Do not give into the temptation to compare your spouse to someone else, or your marriage to other marriages.

Mark 10:8 And they two shall be one flesh: so then they are no more two, but one flesh.

Colossians 3:18-1 Wives, submit yourselves to your own husbands, as it is fit in the Lord. Husbands, love your wives, and be not bitter against them.

You don't know the full story of anyone else's situation, and you are likely to be deceived by them. In the days of Noah, all the animals were supposed to go the ark, some were faster and others were slow yet still they all went in. in this life and in our marriages everyone have different times to reach their destination so stop comparing your situations with others and be content with what you have. Your husband may not have enough money for the home but may be good in sex or he takes good care of you very well, why then would you compare your marriage with someone else's thinking that person's husband or wife is handsome or beautiful and tall and wealthy so that was what you wanted. Oh! Perhaps this man is so weak in bed that if you were to marry him you will end up cheating on him. Or you think the other has too much money and you are wishing it for yourself, listen lady you will end up being beaten by him and the marriage would break apart. Be wise and show contentment with what you have chosen; it is the best.

Husbands and wives remember, in Noah's days some animals were bigger and faster than others yet when they got into the boat they still had to wait for the slower ones before the rains came. So don't let another woman or man influence you stupidly against your own wife or home, you will destroy it with your own hands and then what do you have left; nothing. Don't exchange your joy for unnecessary influences from backgrounds, friends, finance, education, positions, etc. remember two makes a team so it will take your perseverance with patience and understanding to gradually get there whiles you are not giving up. Please know that amongst those who take off in life there are those who seem to be fast pacers and promising but sometimes they do not get to the finished line. There are also those who take the race of life with seriousness and along the line they get distracted and lose focus and then they drop out.

Notice the fastest killers of marriages:

- Pride- as soon as one spouse starts thinking that he or she is better than the other the boat will begin to sink in the marriage because that is the start of trouble. Pride goes before destruction, and a haughty spirit before a fall (Proverbs 16:18). You should know that you are two different persons with different backgrounds coming together to be as one so that the imperfect must join together to become perfect as one and during this process, you both will be tried through fire to melt together like two different metals melted and joined together as one. As a result of this the both of you can now be able to think and agree on decision making. But if there is no humility and tolerance between the two, the trouble would be huge and there would be a mismatch because both of you would not be equally balanced and both of you would get tired of each other in the end. You should be able to build up and tolerate each other to have a happy marriage.

- Learn to show appreciation towards each other – saying thank you, sorry, and laughing a lot at home makes your man or woman stay with you. Nobody want to enter a gloomy place but a place full of laughter will make people want to stay more. So let your spouse feel appreciated in his or her little efforts and that will grow the friendship a lot. Don't let bitterness and pride ruin you and your marriage. Sometimes the thought we have in the marriage nobody knows but God has already seen what our imaginations towards each other are and He Judges. So let us come to our senses and accept each other as we

are and work together for the one common goal of success instead.
- Let us stop irritating ourselves- we should choose to tolerate each other's actions. Sometimes keeping quiet and laughing it off helps you yourself. And let us learn to let things that trouble us go quickly otherwise you will end up being sick. A quote of Billy Graham- no person with an evil imagination can inherit the Kingdom of God. God hates evil imaginations. They lead to habits, habits lead to bondage, and bondage leads to death: "The wages of sin is death" (Romans 6:23).

1 Peter 3:8-11 Finally, all of you, have unity of mind, sympathy, brotherly love, a tender heart, and a humble mind. Do not repay evil for evil or reviling for reviling, but on the contrary, bless, for to this you were called, that you may obtain a blessing. For "Whoever desires to love life and see good days, let him keep his tongue from evil and his lips from speaking deceit; let him turn away from evil and do good; let him seek peace and pursue it.

"Be ye angry, and sin not: let not the sun go down upon your wrath." - Ephesians 4:26,

- Let us learn to forgive ourselves easily – how can you be fighting with your own self. If you can't forgive the other how do you want to be free and also be forgiven? If you forgive easily when it is your turn you won't be scared to ask for it.

"Forbearing one another, and forgiving one another, if any man have a quarrel against any: even as Christ forgave you, so also do ye. And above all these things put on charity, which is the bond of perfectness." - Colossians 3:13-14

- Let us avoid selfishness- put your spouse needs before yours and achieving it for him or her will bring your own happiness out. Work out your own needs too with your spouse when necessary, sharing your troubles builds that strong trust between you.
- Stop trying to be mind readers in the marriage thinking the other should have known what you were thinking, otherwise you will take offense with each other unnecessarily; instead learn to communicate your needs to deepen the trust between the both of you.

- Let us open our eyes and take in all the beauty around us. Even during the worst times there is still much to be thankful for
- We should never forget to have fun in our family because success means nothing without happiness
- Even though we are our husband's helper we should still ask questions when needed; it builds the home. But let us try to avoid acting on suspicion; it breaks the trust between the two and brings about separations

Chapter Five

Respect Your Womanhood

1 Corinthians 11:11-12, Nevertheless, in the Lord woman is not independent of man nor man of woman; for as woman was made from man, so man is now born of woman. And all things are from God.

1 Corinthians 11:8-9, For man was not made from woman, but woman from man. Neither was man created for woman, but woman for man.

Proverbs 14:1, The wisest of women builds her house, but folly with her own hands tears it down.

1 Timothy 2:9-10

Likewise also that women should adorn themselves in respectable apparel, with modesty and self-control, not with braided hair and gold or pearls or costly attire, but with what is proper for women who profess godliness—with good works.

We are women and rightfully yes we are- we came from the man and yet we give birth to the man and so in the end we should know that we are made for each other. That is why when the two meets there is an attraction between opposite sex because there is a dependency between both.

We are our husbands crown and we shine on them we are hires of the grace with our husband in the Lord that is why when they hurt us their prayers are hindered. So let us use our charm of respect to gracefully prepare the road of peace for our husbands so that they can say that we are the bone of their bone and the flesh of their flesh.

Most kings are raised as symbol of authority and pride of the people or nation and in my opinion, our own husband is our king and our pride and he commands that symbol of authority to give us a standard in public. Because of his name and personality we are not looked down in society, among family members, workers, etc. certain backgrounds of our husbands make others give us the respect needed though we may not have earned it alone on our part.

- In our dressing and adornment- let us not dress like prostitutes showing all our body to other men. Come on respect your husband's property. How can you share yourself with more men in addition to your husband because of the way you are dressed? So let us rather adorn ourselves with modesty and good works to shine as the proper crown on our husband's heads. So that they can command the respect wherever they go. If you show your nakedness to another man while claiming you have dressed properly, how do you want to be respected? And how do you want others to respect your husband? Your way of adornment only invite sex from your onlookers. Don't mess up the marriage bed or else you will be destroyed.

- ➢ Stop being naked- stop sharing your problems with everybody inviting unnecessary spirits and advises into your home. Look all that glitters is not gold you are too transparent letting others see your husband or wife's weaknesses. They would tell you what to do and they will live your life for you. There are no proper advice from the jealous and envious ones. There are those who mean to harm you and this would be a proper opportunity for them to do it through conceited smiles and some of the so called friends even want what you have; let

us be careful as women and do the talking on our knees through prayer.
➢ These are our powers that we hold in the home and in ourselves in times of trouble

- Control yourself in times of trouble
- Control your mind and thoughts of negativities
- Be positive in your speech
- Keep yourself busy at home not through gossips but doing something profitable or helping others
- In time of trouble learn to be submissive to discover the solutions
- Don't give yourself to unpleasant pleasures; you would be destroyed by these

- Stop all comparisons and competitions; this would cloud your judgement.
- Seek things that are good and helpful to your home.
- Watch your temper; don't talk nastily to your husband either at home or publicly.
- Show kindness in the home and to others
- Start doing things that will build your home and stop doing things that tears down your home
- Refrain from all quarrels sometimes silence is a weapon
- All nagging should cease and embrace your husband including his weaknesses
- This is the time you use your ability to channel the course of affairs being firm and in humility

- Remaining open-minded brings about new possibilities so try to learn something new every day and you will grow in knowledge
- Know that no matter how bad things seem to be they will always get better
- Let love fill your heart instead of hate. When hate is in your heart here sis no room for anything else but when love is in your heart there is room for endless happiness.

➢ Cover your husband's or wife's nakedness- so he or she made a mess; do you have to tell everybody? Don't you know that the more people know about the other's mess, the more you are exposing your own shame too? We are all not the same in wisdom and understanding, in problem solving and the likes so let us exercise patience and tolerance towards each other.

Why are we always the first to throw stones at our spouse's faults? Let me tell you if you throw a ball to the wall it will bounce back to you. The way you handle matters will either bring grace to you in public or bring shame to you in public. Don't you know that when you cover each other's nakedness it becomes difficult for enemies to attack? Mocking each other brings about anger and through that anger leads you to attack; your shame is now exposed to the world. "Is this how this person is?" somebody will say – I thought he or she was a respectable one. Your nakedness is there for all to see.

Chapter Six

Woman as a Mother

Finally husband, you made your woman into a mother

Mother is a woman who has raised a child, given birth to a child or supplied the egg which in union with a sperm grew into a child. This is the most beautiful experience that a woman can have in her life and sometimes the most stressful. A mother performs so many tasks in different aspects of her life and for her family.

She takes care of her spouse, children, business, social life and health; yet she has been blessed with the power to handle all this numerous affairs at the same time.

A mother is usually the foundation that a home is built upon

- Providing a home firstly for her husband by procreating and handling the homely affairs like cooking
- She provides safe and secure environment in which the children can grow and flourish and develop their personalities
- She serves as a role model and teaches proper manners to the child since she

is the first and closest person the child gets to know.

Proverbs 31:26-27 she opens her mouth with wisdom, and the teaching of kindness is on her tongue. She looks well to the ways of her household and does not eat the bread of idleness.

Isaiah 66:13 as a mother comforts her child, so will I comfort you; and your will be comforted over Jerusalem

Our focus here is comfort which is linking a mother to her child.

A mother's comfort is kind, tender and affectionate; when a child hurts him/herself and is crying, she takes him up in her arms, hugs him/her to her bosom and speaks softly and comfortably to him/her to still and quiet the child. Sometimes she even rubs or blow on it as a way to soothe the child.

Moreover when a mother has a child or person in trouble, she yearns in her heart and does all she can to comfort them or if possible find solutions to the problems.

When a child misbehaves, the mother acts cautiously towards the child and moves herself at a distance, when the child takes notice of, the child takes it to heart, and then as it affects the child she returns to the child and comforts the child.

In proverbs 31:25-30 it says strength and honor are her clothing

A mother shows strength, not through her body but through her mind and actions therefore she is able to bear and do all things with a determination of mind to withstand every enemy or obstacle and persevere till she achieves that aim or goal.

In times of hardship she purposes in her mind and withstands all hardships that stands in her face and works hard to fend for her children.

A mother also gives the right teachings to her children and not manipulate them for her greed or against each other. There is no peace in such a mother's home and all her children run away and leave her in her old age. Just because you gave birth to them does not give you the right to do this to them.

Chapter Seven

Family Limitations

The man and the woman who met and agreed to be one in marriage all come from a different background and usually there are certain negativities that are found in each of this individual family backgrounds. These negativities usually chases them everywhere they go.

We usually neglect these challenges in our lives and think that they are normal but no they are not because these influence our choices, activities and actions in the marriage. There are some families too who have their members scared of leaving their comfort zones including their ill- gotten monies, big houses etc. to allow their marriage to enjoy some peace.

Eg. If your husband or wife has a background where his daddy beats his mom it affects him and he or she usually exhibits this action in the marriage.

Or in a family where the wife's background has the mother disrespecting her husband she naturally picks that attitude and take it to her marriage.

A family where divorce seems to be the order of the day, the children end up practicing the same thing.

We should not neglect these aspects of our lives and begin to deal with them through prayer and counselling before and after we enter into the marriage.

Let us look at this:

Then Abraham complained to Abimelech about a well of water that Abimelech's servants had seized. But Abimelech said, "I don't know who has done this. You did not tell me, and I heard about it only today." Genesis 21:25-26

He replied, "Accept these seven lambs from my hand as a witness that I dug this well." So that place was called Beersheba, because the two men swore an oath there. Genesis 21:30-31

So all the wells that his father's servants had dug in the time of his father Abraham, the Philistines stopped up, filling them with earth. Then Abimelech said to Isaac, "Move away from us; you have become too powerful for us." Genesis 26:15-16

So Isaac moved away from there and encamped in the Valley of Gerar, where he settled. Isaac reopened the wells that had been dug in the time of his father Abraham, which the Philistines had stopped up after Abraham died, and he gave them the same names his father had given them. Genesis 26:17-18

Isaac's servants dug in the valley and discovered a well of fresh water there. But the herders of Gerar quarreled with those of Isaac and said, "The water is ours!" So he

named the well Esek (argument), because they disputed with him. Then they dug another well, but they quarreled over that one also; so he named it Sitnah (hostility). He moved on from there and dug another well, and no one quarreled over it. He named it Rehoboth (open space), saying, "Now the Lord has given us room and we will flourish in the land."
Genesis 26:19-22

Notice Abraham experienced Abimelech servants' arguments over a well so was Isaac his son too. Abraham had to say that his wife was his sister and Isaac did the same too. (Genesis 26:1-35)

Mark 3:27, "But no one can enter the strong man's house and plunder his property unless he first binds the strong man, and then he will plunder his house.

The things and issues that takes place in our families usually follow us into our own success therefore before we can be delivered from them we first of all have to identify what bothers us in the marriage. Is it cheating, beating up our spouse, being irresponsible, stealing etc. if we can identify what needs to be changed then we can fight it. Otherwise how can we fight what is hidden?

Jeremiah 31:11, For the LORD has ransomed Jacob and redeemed him from the hand of him who was stronger than he

What fights us is sometimes stronger than us so we need to pray to the Lord fervently and accept that we do not want these troubles anymore, then wait patiently for the deliverance from the Lord. Also know that despite the challenges and obstacles you are passing through and the once ahead of you God will take you through and bring you the place He has destined for you but you have to believe and never give up.

- ➢ We should desire that we do not want this limitation again to set the pace for change
- ➢ We should believe that Jesus Christ is the only way to the solutions
- ➢ Delve into the word of God and look for similar situations or ask for verses that match up your problem and meditate on them
- ➢ Ignore negative voices in your head. Focus instead on the goal set and remember your previous accomplishments. Your past successes are your stepping stones to rise up for your future

- Speak onto the problem because there is power in your mouth and in the words that you say.
- Break away from the habits that stands and lead you to sin and have hope that you will accomplish what you have set your mind to achieve
- Decide that you will be successful and happy and good things will find you. believe the road blocks and obstacles along the way are only minor
- Create friendship in the family so that you can share your troubles, hope, dreams, sorrow and happiness together.
- Learn to forgive- holding grudges would only weigh you down and inspire unhappiness and grief. Rise above it and remember that everyone makes mistakes

- Grow up and leave the childhood monsters behind and believe that they can no longer hurt or stand in your way
- Keep hoping for the best and never forget that anything is possible as long as you remain dedicated to the task

Chapter Eight

Our Focus in Marriage

Genesis 3:6-7, ⁶When the woman saw that the fruit of the tree was good for food and pleasing to the eye, and also desirable for gaining wisdom, she took some and ate it. She also gave some to her husband, who was with her, and he ate it. ⁷Then the eyes of both of them were opened, and they realized they were naked; so they sewed fig leaves together and made coverings for themselves.

We realize that the focus of the woman changed when she started paying attention to the fruit, and she began to desire what she was looking at to the point of eating it. Her focus was no more on the agreement between her husband and God but on something else that someone was telling her about. Because of this her control was lost. So my question is:

In your marriage what do you focus on and what are you focusing on at the moment? Is your focus on hate, anger, silly mistakes of the other partner, on your children, work, friends, unnecessary habits, persecutions, trials, temptations, hardship etc. then I am telling you that:

Matthew 6:21, For where your treasure is, there your heart will be also.

Initially, there was only one option i.e. they leaned on God's command but then the choices became two and she chose the second option and that brought trouble. When there are too many things to choose from our control to make the right choice or decision get shaken. That is why it takes that team effort of the husband and wife to make the decision together. In the decision making for the future of both there should be lots of questions asked so that all loop holes can be sealed. There should also be shared talents, skills, knowledge and time with each other because all these investments will return multiples of blessing and a cordial love that set as the foundation of the marriage.

When our focus on God is shifted, the marriage becomes shaken. So Jesus said look unto me the author and the finisher of your faith. Let us not shift our focus from God.

Also when the initial plan of love between the two in the marriage is changed the marriage suffer consequences. We should learn to discipline ourselves in the marriage instead of allowing people and things, attitudes to manipulate us. Sometimes in the marriage when couples are tired, they should relax or take a break to have fun and allow time knowing that things would always have a way of working itself out and trust God to give you strength as you walk through that storm. Sharing similarities in character also help to achieve our goals easily in the marriage but when each other have a different view point, sometimes it is not helpful and does not promote peace in the home. Each one becomes vulnerable to their emotions and gets scared of being hurt again so each tries to manage their feelings against the other instead of freely expressing it to feel the joy the marriage.

Chapter Nine

Conclusion

In conclusion let us enjoy our marriage to the fullest and avoid the unnecessary stuff if possible.

Song of Solomon 2:15- Take us the foxes, the little foxes, that spoil the vines: for our vines have tender grapes

Song of Solomon 2 King James Version (KJV)

2 I am the rose of Sharon, and the lily of the valleys.

² As the lily among thorns, so is my love among the daughters.

³ As the apple tree among the trees of the wood, so is my beloved among the sons. I sat down under his shadow with great delight, and his fruit was sweet to my taste.

⁴ He brought me to the banqueting house, and his banner over me was love.

⁵ Stay me with flagons, comfort me with apples: for I am sick of love.

⁶ His left hand is under my head, and his right hand doth embrace me.

⁷ I charge you, O ye daughters of Jerusalem, by the roes, and by the hinds of the field, that ye stir not up, nor awake my love, till he please.

⁸ The voice of my beloved! behold, he cometh leaping upon the mountains, skipping upon the hills.

⁹ My beloved is like a roe or a young hart: behold, he standeth behind our wall, he looketh forth at the windows, shewing himself through the lattice.

¹⁰ My beloved spake, and said unto me, Rise up, my love, my fair one, and come away.

¹¹ For, lo, the winter is past, the rain is over and gone;

¹² The flowers appear on the earth; the time of the singing of birds is come, and the voice of the turtle is heard in our land;

¹³ The fig tree putteth forth her green figs, and the vines with the tender grape give a good smell. Arise, my love, my fair one, and come away.

¹⁴ O my dove, that art in the clefts of the rock, in the secret places of the stairs, let me see thy countenance, let me hear thy voice; for sweet is thy voice, and thy countenance is comely.

¹⁵ Take us the foxes, the little foxes, that spoil the vines: for our vines have tender grapes.

¹⁶ My beloved is mine, and I am his: he feedeth among the lilies.

¹⁷ Until the day break, and the shadows flee away, turn, my beloved, and be thou like a roe or a young hart upon the mountains of Bether

Set me as a seal upon thine heart, as a seal upon thine arm: for love is strong as death; jealousy is cruel as the grave: the coals thereof are coals of fire, which hath a most vehement flame.

⁷ Many waters cannot quench love, neither can the floods drown it: if a man would give all the substance of his house for love, it would utterly be contemned.

www.ingramcontent.com/pod-product-compliance
Lightning Source LLC
Chambersburg PA
CBHW020126130526
44591CB00032B/544